What Is in the Sky?

Laura Young

Rosen REAL READERS

Rosen Classroom Books & Materials
New York

What is in the sky?

The Sun is in the sky.

The Moon is in the sky.

Stars are in the sky.

Clouds are in the sky.

Birds fly in the sky!

Words to Know

birds

clouds

Moon

stars

Sun